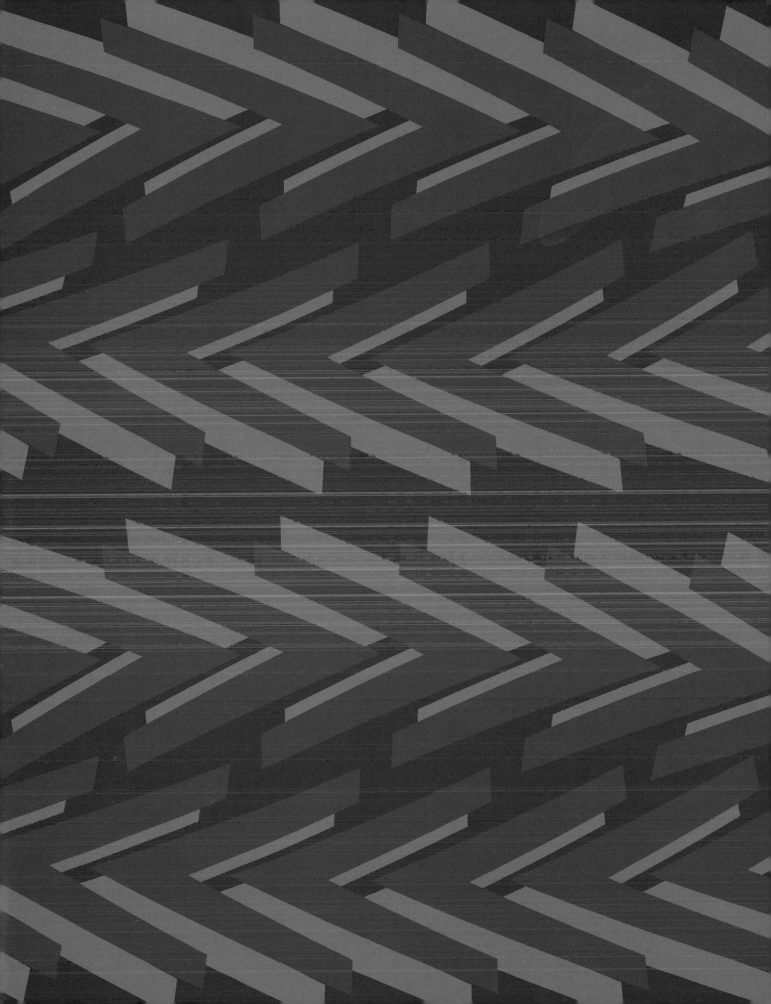

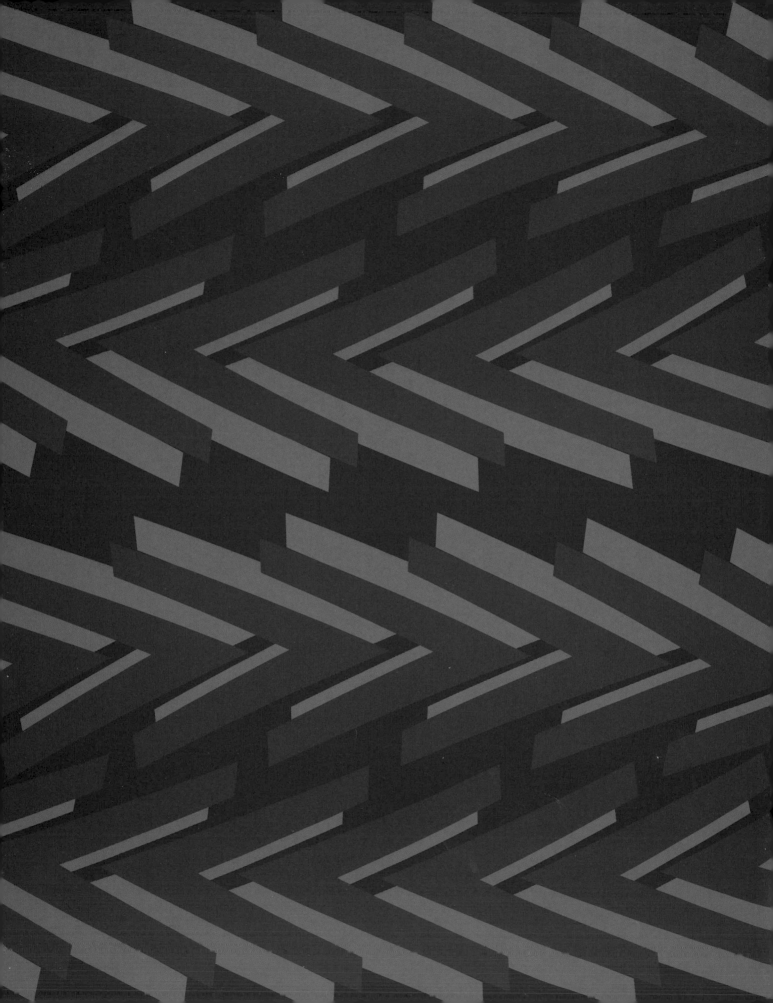

This is my racing car

Written by Chris Oxlade
Photography by Andy Crawford

SEA-TO-SEA
Mankato Collingwood London

This edition first published in 2008 by
Sea-to-Sea Publications
1980 Lookout Drive
North Mankato
Minnesota 56003

Printed in China

Library of Congress Cataloging in Publication Data:

Oxlade, Chris.
   This is my racing car / by Chris Oxlade.
      p.cm. -- (Mega machine drivers)
   Includes index.
   ISBN 978-1-59771-107-4
    1. Automobile racing--Juvenile literature. I. Title.

GV1029.13.O95 2007
796.72--dc22

                              2006052867

9 8 7 6 5 4 3 2

Published by arrangement with the Watts Publishing Group Ltd, London.

Editor: Jennifer Schofield
Designer: Jemima Lumley
Photography: Andy Crawford
Racing car driver: Rodolfo Gonzalez

Acknowledgments:
Jakob Ebrey: p21; p23; p24; p25; p27
The Publisher would like to thank Russell Eacott, Rodolfo Gonzalez,
Olly Smith, and all at T-Sport for their help producing this book.

▶ Contents

> Me and my racing car

Hello! This mega machine is a racing car. I am a racing car driver.

▽ *I drive my car in races.*
My car is very, very fast.

> Racing car power

My racing car is pushed along by an engine.

∧ *The engine is under the engine cover.*

> *To see the engine, the mechanic takes off the engine cover.*

> The engine
needs fuel to
make it work.
The fuel goes
in here.

> Wheels and tires

The engine makes the back wheels go around. The wheels push the car along the track.

The tires are wide. They stop the car from sliding around on the race track.

◀ *This tire is for dry weather.*

◀ *This tire is for rainy weather. The grooves help the tire to grip the track.*

◀ *The mechanic has taken off the tire to check the brakes. I use the brakes to slow the car down.*

brake

> The bodywork

My car is covered with smooth bodywork. It lets the car go quickly.

The mechanic lifts off some of the bodywork to fix the parts underneath.

This piece of bodywork is called the nose cone.

> The wings

The wings press the car down as it zooms along. This helps the tires grip the track.

The rear wing presses the back tires down.

The front wing presses the front tires down.

# The cockpit

I sit in the cockpit. It is full of controls for driving the car.

I press buttons on the steering wheel when I want to go faster or slower.

▽ *I take the steering wheel off to get in and out of the cockpit.*

> Ready to drive

I wear special clothes when I drive my car. They keep me safe if in case I have an accident.

> My racing suit, gloves, and shoes are all fireproof.

< My helmet protects my head. Inside are headphones for the team radio.

The mechanic does up my harness and puts on my steering wheel. I am ready to drive!

> Testing and practice

I am part of a big team
that races the car.

∧ When I test drive the car,
I tell the mechanics if there
are things that need to be fixed.

▽ *In the days before a race, I practice driving around the track.*

▶ At the race

Today is race day!

▲ *My car is taken to the race track in a big truck.*

▲ *I have to drive really quickly to overtake the other cars.*

◀ *The race is over when the black-and-white flag is waved.*

> More racing cars

Here are some more
racing cars that I drive.

△ *This is a kart. My first
racing car was a kart.*

▽ *This is a touring car. It is like the cars you see on the road, but it goes much faster!*

> Be a racing car driver

It takes a lot of hard work to become a racing car driver.

You have to learn about the different parts of the car.

▽ You have to practice driving the car for hours and hours to learn to drive fast and safely.

> Racing car parts

helmet

rear wing

cockpit

wheel

nose cone

front wing

> Word bank

bodywork—the metal part of the car that covers things such as the engine

cockpit—where the driver sits

engine—the part of a racing car that makes it move

fireproof—something that will not catch fire

harness—the strap that keeps drivers in the cockpit

mechanic—the person who fixes the racing car

team radio—the special radio that lets a driver talk to his team while he is racing

rear—back

Websites

This racing car is from the T-Sport Formula 3 team. To find out more about the car and the driver, Rodolfo Gonzalez, log on to www.t-sportgroup.com

Index

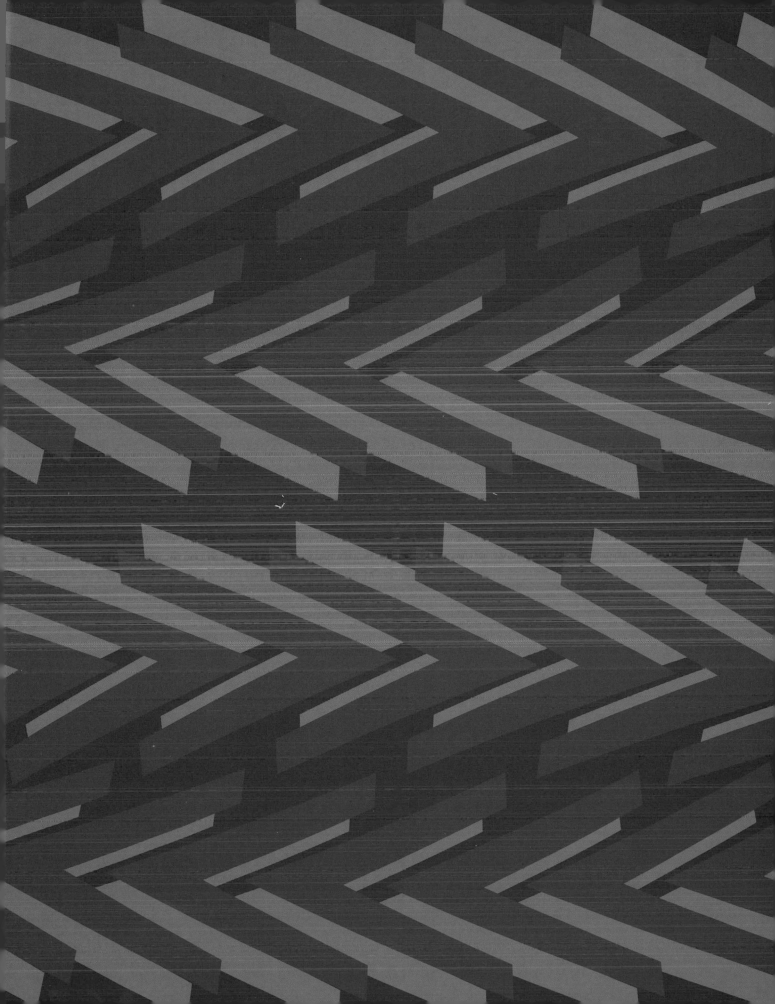